Thank You

FOR BEING MY

Father

Thank You

FOR BEING MY

Father

The quoted ideas expressed in this book (but not scripture verses) are not, in all cases, exact quotations, as some have been edited for clarity and brevity. In all cases, the author has attempted to maintain the speaker's original intent. In some cases, quoted material for this book was obtained from secondary sources, primarily print media. While every effort was made to ensure the accuracy of these sources, the accuracy cannot be guaranteed. For additions, deletions, corrections, or clarifications in future editions of this text, please contact Paul Shepherd, Executive Director for Elm Hill Books. Email pshepherd@elmhillbooks.com.

Scripture quotations are taken from:

The Holy Bible, New King James Version (NKJV) Copyright © 1982 by Thomas Nelson, Inc. Used by permission.

New Century Version (NCV) © 1987, 1988, 1991 by Word Publishing, a division of Thomas Nelson, Inc. All rights reserved. Used by permission.

Cover Design by Denise Rosser
Page Layout by Bart Dawson

ISBN 1-4041-8512-7

Printed in the United States of America

To My Father

CONTENTS

INTRODUCTION

Because you're reading this book, you probably answer to the name Dad, Daddy, Pop, Father, or some variation thereof. If so, congratulations: Few of life's joys can match the glorious responsibility of raising your family *and* leading it. As a dedicated dad, you know that parenting is hard work—*lots* of hard work. But you also know that the rewards of fatherhood are far too numerous to count.

George Herbert observed, "One father equals a hundred schoolmasters." How true. As a responsible parent, you *have* taught and *will continue* to teach life's most important lessons. Many of those lessons are contained in this book.

The Bible verses and quotations on these pages remind us that a father, as he leads his family, places his mark upon eternity. And we children are eternally grateful.

Thank You for...

BEING MY FATHER

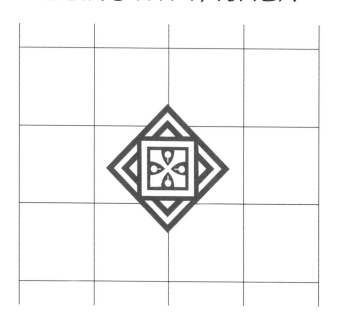

The righteous man walks in his integrity;
His children are blessed after him.

PROVERBS 20:7 NKJV

DEAR DAD,

Thank you for being my father. Thanks for the love, the care, the work, the discipline, the motivation, the wisdom, the support, and the faith. Thanks for being a concerned parent and a worthy example. Thanks for giving life and teaching it. Thanks for being patient with me, even when you were tired, or frustrated—or both. And thanks for being a man who is worthy of admiration *and* love.

You deserve my thanks, Dad, but you deserve so much more. You deserve our family's undying gratitude. You deserve happiness, contentment, praise, and peace. May you enjoy God's blessings always, and may you never, ever forget how much we love you.

Signed,
Your Loving Child

A FATHER'S HAND
MOLDS THE FAMILY,
SHAPES THE WORLD,
AND REFASHIONS
ETERNITY.

∽

MARIE T. FREEMAN

Fatherhood is pretending that
the gift you love most is soap-on-a-rope.

BILL COSBY

Life doesn't come with an instruction book;
that's why we have fathers.

H. JACKSON BROWN

A father is someone who carries pictures
where his money used to be.

ANONYMOUS

How badly America needs husbands and fathers
who are committed to their families, men who
are determined to succeed
in this important responsibility.

JAMES DOBSON

Money can build or buy a house.
Add love to that, and you have a home.
Add God to that, and you have a temple.
You have "a little colony
of the kingdom of heaven."

ANNE ORTLAND

In the presence of love, miracles happen.

ROBERT SCHULLER

No other structure can replace the family.
Without it, our children have
no moral foundation. Without it,
they become moral illiterates
whose only law is self.

CHUCK COLSON

Children are not so different from kites.
Children were created to fly. But, they need wind
and strength that comes from unconditional
love, encouragement, and prayer.

GIGI GRAHAM TCHIVIDJIAN

Kids go where there is excitement.
They stay where there is love.

ZIG ZIGLAR

All children have the right to a daddy
who is rational and sound and who shows
his love by the way he treats them.

JERRY CLOWER

You have to love your children unselfishly.
That's hard. But it's the only way.

BARBARA BUSH

Real love has staying power.
Authentic love is tough love.
It refuses to look for ways to run away.
It always opts for working through.

CHARLES SWINDOLL

My father is the standard by which all
subsequent men in my life have been judged.

KATHRYN MCCARTHY GRAHAM

Line by line, moment by moment, special times
are etched into our memories in
the permanent ink of everlasting love
in our relationships.

GLORIA GAITHER

When the whole family is together,
the soul is in place.

RUSSIAN PROVERB

What can we do to promote world peace?
Go home and love your family.

MOTHER TERESA

He is happiest, be he king or peasant,
who finds his peace in his home.

GOETHE

He knew without a doubt that in wife
and child he had the only treasures
that really mattered anyway.

LEWIS GRIZZARD

THE BEST USE
OF LIFE IS LOVE.
THE BEST EXPRESSION
OF LOVE IS TIME.
THE BEST TIME
TO LOVE IS NOW.

RICK WARREN

Thank You for . . .
YOUR TIME

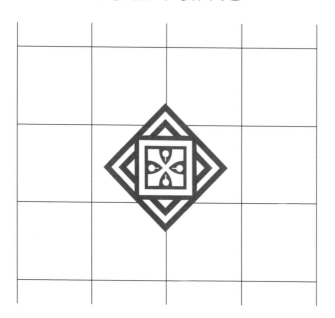

To everything there is a season,
a time for every purpose under heaven.

ECCLESIASTES 3:1 NKJV

DEAR DAD,

You were never too busy for me—thank you for your time. When I had a problem, you listened. When I scraped a knee, you provided the bandage. When I needed help with my homework, you pitched in. When I spoke a single line in the class play, you sat on the first row—and smiled. Whatever I did and wherever I did it, you were right there in my corner, cheering me on—and I noticed.

As you know all too well, Dad, time is a precious thing, a priceless treasure that should never be squandered. You gave me *so much* of your time that words simply can't express what it meant to me then . . . *and now.*

DO YOU LOVE LIFE?
THEN DO NOT
SQUANDER TIME,
FOR THAT'S THE STUFF
LIFE IS MADE OF.

✑

BEN FRANKLIN

Children just don't fit into a "to do" list
very well. It takes time to be an effective parent
when children are small. It takes time to
introduce them to good books—it takes time
to fly kites and play punch ball and
put together jigsaw puzzles.
It takes time to listen.

JAMES DOBSON

I have decided not to let my time be used up
by people to whom I make no difference
while I neglect those for whom
I am irreplaceable.

TONY CAMPOLO

I DON'T BUY THE CLICHÉ
THAT QUALITY TIME
IS THE MOST
IMPORTANT THING.
IF YOU DON'T HAVE
ENOUGH QUANTITY,
YOU WON'T GET QUALITY.

LEIGHTON FORD

It takes time to be a good father.
It takes effort trying, failing, and trying again.

TIM HANSEL

There is so much to teach,
and the time goes so fast.

ERMA BOMBECK

Prime-time parents are parents who consider
every minute with their children
a prime time to communicate the message of
parental love, interest, and care.

KAY KUZMA

When we love something it is of value to us,
and when something is of value to us
we spend time with it, time enjoying it,
and time taking care of it. Got a minute?
So it is when we love children:
we spend time admiring them and
taking care of them.
We give them our time.

M. SCOTT PECK

If you've found yourself breathlessly chasing
the guy in front to you, break free.
Spend some time with your family.
Take a walk with someone you love.
Hold a three-year-old on your lap and
tell him or her a story. Life is simply too short
to be spent plodding around in endless circles.

JAMES DOBSON

Many things we need can wait. The child cannot.
Now is the time his bones are being formed;
his blood is being made;
his mind is being developed.
to him we cannot say tomorrow.
His name is today.

GABRIELA MISTRAL

To those who would say,
"We don't have time to do these things!"
I would say,
"You don't have time not to!"

STEPHEN COVEY

Thank You for . . .
YOUR EXAMPLE

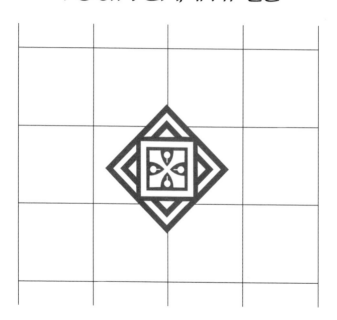

Be an example to the believers in word,
in conduct, in love, in spirit, in faith, in purity.

1 TIMOTHY 4:12 NKJV

DEAR DAD,

Thanks for the example you've set. You have taught me some of life's most important lessons, not only by your words but also by your actions. You weren't always perfect—nobody is—but when you did make mistakes, you corrected them, and you moved on.

Your life has been a living lesson in the importance of character. I have been blessed by your example, and I'll happily spend the rest of my life trying, as best I can, to live up to the standards you have set.

AN OUNCE OF
FATHER'S EXAMPLE
IS WORTH A POUND
OF FATHER'S ADVICE.

MARIE T. FREEMAN

The power of example in a parent does more
to train a child than any other single thing.

LARRY CHRISTENSON

We are effective only when we have integrity,
when our actions are in line with our values.

STEPHEN COVEY

If you want to be successful at helping others,
demonstrate that you can make
your philosophy work in your own life.

NAPOLEON HILL

In matters of principle, stand like a rock;
in matters of taste, swim with the current.

THOMAS JEFFERSON

The life of a good person ought to abound
in every virtue so that he is, on the interior,
what to others he appears to be.

THOMAS À KEMPIS

I believe that it is always more powerful
to live out your values than to preach them.

RICH DEVOS

Integrity of heart is indispensable.

JOHN CALVIN

What you do speaks so loudly
that I cannot hear what you say.

RALPH WALDO EMERSON

Try not to become men of success.
Rather, become men of value.

ALBERT EINSTEIN

If the rascals knew the advantage of virtue,
they would become honest men.

BEN FRANKLIN

Character is like a tree and reputation
like its shadow. The shadow is what we think;
the tree is the real thing.

ABRAHAM LINCOLN

If I take care of my character,
my reputation will take care of itself.

D. L. MOODY

Character is formed by doing the thing
we are supposed to do, when it should be done,
whether we feel like doing it or not.

FATHER FLANAGAN

Sow an action, you reap a habit; sow a habit,
you reap a character; sow a character,
you reap a destiny.

FRANCES E. WILLARD

Expedients are for the hour;
principles for the ages.

HENRY WARD BEECHER

Example is not the main thing
in influencing others—it is the only thing.

ALBERT SCHWEITZER

Character is made in the small moments
of our lives.

PHILLIPS BROOKS

There is no way to grow a saint overnight.
Character, like the oak tree,
does not spring up like a mushroom.

VANCE HAVNER

He or she is greatest who contributes
the greatest original practical example.

WALT WHITMAN

Life is not easy for any of us. But it is a continual challenge, and it is up to us to be cheerful and to be strong, so that those who depend on us may draw strength from our example.

ROSE KENNEDY

You cannot not model. It's impossible. People will see your example, positive or negative, as a pattern for the way life is lived.

STEPHEN COVEY

One example is worth a thousand arguments.

THOMAS CARLYLE

LET YOUR LIFE SPEAK.

QUAKER SAYING

Thank You for . . .

YOUR
ENCOURAGEMENT

Let us think about each other
and help each other to show love
and do good deeds.

HEBREWS 10:24 NCV

DEAR DAD,

Thanks for the encouragement. Even when I did not believe in myself, you believed in me . . . and it showed.

Sometimes, I gave up on myself, but you never did. Even on those darker days when I couldn't see hope for the future, you could. Thankfully, you never stopped believing in my abilities, and you never stopped telling me so. Your faith eventually wore off. Now, because of you, I believe in myself. And that, Dad, is the power of encouragement.

ENCOURAGEMENT
IS THE OXYGEN
OF THE SOUL.

JOHN MAXWELL

Never discourage anyone who continually
makes progress, no matter how slow.

PLATO

My primary role as father is not to be
the boss and just look good, but to be
a servant leader who enables and
enhances my family to be their best.

TIM HANSEL

For every one of us who succeeds,
it's because there's somebody
there to show us the way.

OPRAH WINFREY

The balance of affirmation and discipline,
freedom and restraint, encouragement and
warning is different for each child and season
and generation, yet the absolutes of God's Word
are necessary and trustworthy at all times.

GLORIA GAITHER

Kids really respond to praise and encouragement.
I try to praise my kids at least
twenty-five times a day.

JOSH MCDOWELL

Discouraged people don't need critics.
They hurt enough already. What they need
is encouragement. They need a refuge,
a willing, caring, available someone.

CHARLES SWINDOLL

So often we think that to be encouragers
we have to produce great words of wisdom
when, in fact, a few simple syllables of
sympathy and an arm around the shoulder
can often provide much needed comfort.

FLORENCE LITTAUER

There are no words to express the abyss between
isolation and having one ally. It may be conceded
to the mathematician that four is twice two.
But, two is not twice one;
two is two thousand times one.

G. K. CHESTERTON

Those who keep speaking about the sun while
walking under a cloudy sky are messengers of
hope, the true saints of our day.

HENRI J. NOUWEN

Encouragement starts at home,
but it should never end there.

MARIE T. FREEMAN

If someone listens or stretches out a hand
or whispers a word of encouragement
or attempts to understand a lonely person,
extraordinary things begin to happen.

LORETTA GIRZARTIS

Perhaps once in a hundred years a person
may be ruined by excessive praise.
But surely once every minute someone dies
inside for the lack of it.

CECIL G. OSBORNE

A really great person is the person
who makes every person feel great.

G. K. CHESTERTON

Studies have shown that for every negative thing
you say to a child, you must say four positive
things just to keep the balance.

J. ALLAN PETERSEN

It's a father's job to convince his children
that they are gifted.
Ultimately, it's the child's job to use that gift.

J. R. FREEMAN

My father gave me the greatest gift anyone
could give another person: he believed in me.

JIM VALVANO

Never tell a young person that anything
cannot be done. God may have been waiting
centuries for someone ignorant enough
of the impossible to do that very thing.

JOHN ANDREW HOLMES

Words. Do you fully understand their power?
Can any of us really grasp the mighty force
behind the things we say? Do we stop
and think before we speak,
considering the potency of the words we utter?

JONI EARECKSON TADA

It is the nature of man to rise to greatness
if greatness is expected of him.

JOHN STEINBECK

Children have more need of models than critics.

JOSEPH JOUBERT

A lot of people have gone further than
they thought they could because
someone else thought they could.

ZIG ZIGLAR

It is identifying yourself with the hopes, dreams,
fears and longings of others,
that you may understand them
and help them.

WILFERD PETERSON

Everybody wants to be somebody.
The thing you have to do is give them
the confidence that they can become
the kind of people they want to become.

GEORGE FOREMAN

Who is the happiest of men?
He who values the merits of others,
and in their pleasure takes joy,
even as though it were his own.

GOETHE

NINE-TENTHS
OF EDUCATION IS
ENCOURAGEMENT.

ANATOLE FRANCE

Thank You for . . .
A HAPPY HOME

A happy heart is like good medicine.

PROVERBS 17:22 NCV

DEAR DAD,

Thanks for providing a happy home. You showed me that a home is not simply a place; it is a state of mind, built as much with love as with brick and mortar.

The size of a house is relatively unimportant; the collective size of the hearts that dwell inside it is all-important. You made our home a place where we knew we were loved. And we will never forget.

THE SECRET OF A HAPPY HOME LIFE IS THAT THE MEMBERS OF THE FAMILY LEARN TO GIVE AND RECEIVE LOVE.

∽

BILLY GRAHAM

The greatest happiness is found in
the home where God is loved and honored,
where each one loves, and helps,
and cares for the others.

ST. THEOPHANE VENARD

Home is not only where the heart is;
it is also where the happiness is.

MARIE T. FREEMAN

Happiness grows at our own firesides,
and is not to be picked in strangers' gardens.

DOUGLAS JERROLD

You cannot honor your family without nuturing
your own sense of personal value and honor.

STEPHEN COVEY

When you look at your life,
the greatest happiness is family happiness.

JOYCE BROTHERS

The family: We are a strange little band of
characters trudging through life sharing diseases,
toothpaste, coveting one another's desserts,
hiding shampoo, borrowing money,
locking each other out of rooms, loving,
laughing, defending, and trying to figure out
the common thread that
bound us all together.

ERMA BOMBECK

A HAPPY FAMILY IS BUT AN EARLIER HEAVEN.

∽

JOHN BOWRING

Well, I hope that while I live I may keep my
"Old fashioned" theories, and that, at least,
in my own family, I may continue to feel that
home is the best and happiest place, and
that my son and daughter and their children
will live in peace and keep from the tarnish
which seems to affect so many.

SARA DELANO ROOSEVELT

The happiest moments of my life have been
the few which I have passed at home
in the bosom of my family.

THOMAS JEFFERSON

The family is that dear octopus from
whose tentacles we never quite escape,
nor, in our innermost hearts,
ever quite wish to.

DODIE SMITH

FAMILY IS THE WE OF ME.

CARSON MCCULLERS

Thank You for . . .

LISTENING

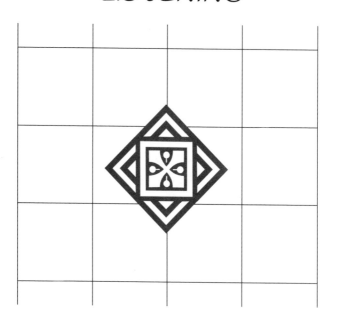

Always be willing to listen and slow to speak.

JAMES 1:19 NCV

DEAR DAD,

Thanks for listening . . . and for trying your best to understand. Sometimes, I'm quite sure that you must have been frustrated by the things that I said and did. But you listened anyway. And sometimes, you understood me far better than I understood myself.

Of course you were willing to share your advice (which, I regret to admit, I sometimes ignored), but you were also willing to let me make my own mistakes without saying, "I told you so."

Even when my words must have seemed silly or repetitive, you kept listening. And that made all the difference.

THE MORE A CHILD
BECOMES AWARE
OF A FATHER'S
WILLINGNESS TO LISTEN,
THE MORE A FATHER
WILL BEGIN TO HEAR.

GEORGE MACDONALD

The first duty of love is to listen.

PAUL TILLICH

Parents need to listen and be patient
as their children talk to them.
A listening ear and a loving ear
always go together.

WARREN WIERSBE

The reason that we have two ears
and only one mouth is that we may listen
the more and talk the less.

ZENO OF CITIUM

It takes a great person to make a good listener.

ARTHUR HELPS

Part of good communication is listening
with the eyes as well as with the ears.

JOSH MCDOWELL

Listening, not imitation,
is the sincerest form of flattery.

JOYCE BROTHERS

Know how to listen,
and you will profit even from those
who talk badly.

PLUTARCH

Listen with sincerity.

JOE GIRARD

People ought to listen more slowly!

JEAN SPARKS DUCEY

The older I grow, the more I listen to people
who don't say much.

GERMAIN G. GLIDDEN

One of the best ways to persuade others
is with your ears—by listening to them.

DEAN RUSK

Sleep not when others speak.

GEORGE WASHINGTON

ALL WISE MEN SHARE
ONE TRAIT IN COMMON:
THE ABILITY TO LISTEN.

FRANK TYGER

Thank You for ...
YOUR LEADERSHIP

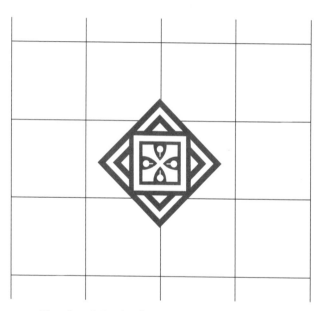

Shepherd God's flock, for whom you are responsible. Watch over them because you want to, not because you are forced. That is how God wants it. Do it because you are happy to serve.

1 PETER 5:2 NCV

DEAR DAD,

Thanks for being the kind of leader I could follow with pride. I needed someone to look up to, and you were a man I could genuinely admire.

When I needed a pat on the back, you patted; when I needed an encouraging word, you spoke up; and when I needed "straight talk," you were always honest and always concerned.

You struck a proper balance between discipline and fun. It could not have been easy, but you made it look easy . . . and that made all the difference.

YOU CAN NEVER
SEPARATE
A LEADER'S ACTIONS
FROM HIS CHARACTER.

JOHN MAXWELL

A man ought to live so that everybody knows
he is a Christian, and most of all,
his family ought to know.

D. L. MOODY

Let us look upon our children;
let us love them and train them as children
of the covenant and children of the promise.
These are the children of God.

ANDREW MURRAY

Happy is the child who happens in upon
his parent from time to time to see him
on his knees, or going aside regularly,
to keep times with the Lord.

LARRY CHRISTENSON

LEADERSHIP IS
A COMBINATION OF
STRATEGY AND
CHARACTER.
IF YOU MUST BE
WITHOUT ONE,
BE WITHOUT
THE STRATEGY.

∽

NORMAN SCHWARZKOPF

People are only too glad to obey
the man who they believe has wiser thoughts
for their interests than they themselves do.

XENOPHON

Greatness lies not in being strong,
but in the right use of strength.

HENRY WARD BEECHER

The strength of the group is the strength
of the leader.

VINCE LOMBARDI

Blessed is the influence of one true,
loving human being upon another.

GEORGE ELIOT

What greater work is there than training
the mind and forming the habits of the young?

ST. JOHN CHRYSOSTOM

Teaching is not the filling of the pale,
but the lighting of the fire.

WILLIAM BUTLER YEATS

BETTER TO INSTRUCT A CHILD THAN TO COLLECT RICHES.

HERVE OF BRITTANY

God wants to make something beautiful
of our lives; our task—as God's children
and as our children's parents—is to let Him.

JIM GALLERY

All the flowers of all the tomorrows
are in the seeds of today.

ANNE OUTLAND

There are two lasting bequests we can hope
to give our children. One of these is roots;
the other, wings.

HODDING CARTER

The imprint of the parent remains forever
on the life of the child.

C. B. EAVEY

Train your child in the way in which you know
you should have gone yourself.

C.H. SPURGEON

One father equals a hundred schoolmasters.

GEORGE HERBERT

Thank You for . . .

YOUR POSITIVE ATTITUDE

Finally, brethren, whatever things are true, whatever things are noble, whatever things are just, whatever things are pure, whatever things are lovely, whatever things are of good report, if there is any virtue and if there is anything praiseworthy—meditate on these things.

PHILIPPIANS 4:8 NKJV

DEAR DAD,

You always seemed to understand that a father's attitude is contagious. If a father is optimistic and upbeat, the family will tend to be likewise. But if a dad ever falls prey to pessimism and doubt, the family suffers right along with him.

Thanks for your positive attitude. When I found myself dwelling on the negatives of life, you helped me count my blessings instead of my troubles. Your optimism was contagious: it gave me the courage to dream . . . and the faith to believe that my dreams can come true.

ENTHUSIASM
INVITES ENTHUSIASM.

RUSSELL CONWELL

The father is the head of a unit of people
launched on an exploration of life and
all the things God has placed in the world
for us to discover and enjoy.

GEORGE MACDONALD

A child's formative years are the most important
for instilling the right attitudes.

JOHN MAXWELL

A positive attitude will have positive results
because attitudes are contagious.

ZIG ZIGLAR

The people whom I have seen succeed best
in life have always been cheerful
and hopeful people who went about
their business with a smile on their faces.

CHARLES KINGSLEY

There is wisdom in the habit of looking
at the bright side of life.

FATHER FLANAGAN

If you can't tell whether your glass is half-empty
of half-full, you don't need another glass;
what you need is better eyesight . . .
and a more thankful heart.

MARIE T. FREEMAN

WHEN YOU AFFIRM BIG,
BELIEVE BIG,
AND PRAY BIG,
BIG THINGS HAPPEN.

NORMAN VINCENT PEALE

Great hopes make great men.

THOMAS FULLER

Positive anything is better than
negative nothing.

ELBERT HUBBARD

No pessimist ever discovered the secrets
of the stars or sailed to an uncharted land,
or opened a new heaven to
the human spirit.

HELEN KELLER

Do not build up obstacles in your imagination.
Difficulties must be studied and dealt with,
but they must not be magnified by fear.

NORMAN VINCENT PEALE

An optimistic mind is a healthy mind.

LORETTA YOUNG

Write it on your heart that every day is
the best day of the year.

RALPH WALDO EMERSON

The hopeful man sees success where others
see failure, sunshine where
others see shadows and storm.

O. S. MARDEN

I've never seen a monument erected
to a pessimist.

PAUL HARVEY

Each of us makes his own weather.

FULTON J. SHEEN

Good thoughts bear good fruit
and bad thoughts bear bad fruit.
And a man is his own gardener.

JAMES ALLEN

THIS IS THE DAY
THE LORD HAS MADE;
WE WILL REJOICE
AND BE GLAD IN IT.

PSALM 118:24 NKJV

Everything can be taken from a man
but one thing: the last of the human freedoms—
to choose one's attitude in any given set of
circumstances, to choose one's own way.

VICTOR FRANKL

An inexhaustible good nature is one of
the most precious gifts of heaven.

WASHINGTON IRVING

There are souls in this world which have
the gift of finding joy everywhere and
of leaving it behind them when they go.

FREDERICK WILLIAM FABER

THE PRESENT MOMENT
IS FILLED WITH JOY
AND HAPPINESS.
IF YOU ARE ATTENTIVE,
YOU WILL SEE IT.

THICH NHAT HANH

Thank You for . . .
YOUR PRAYERS

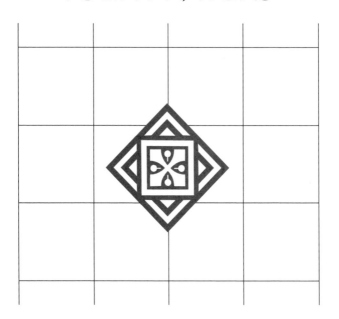

The effective, fervent prayer of
a righteous man avails much.

JAMES 5:16 NKJV

DEAR DAD,

Thank you for your prayers. God most certainly hears those prayers, and I am most certainly blessed by them.

Prayer changes things, and it changes us. As a father whose heart is turned toward God, you know that our Heavenly Father is always listening, and that He wants to hear from us right now. Thank you for the words you have spoken to Him on my behalf. Rest assured that I, too, have quiet conversations with our Creator, and rest assured that I'm praying for you, just as you are praying for me.

PRAYING FOR OUR
CHILDREN IS A NOBLE
TASK. THERE IS NOTHING
MORE SPECIAL,
MORE PRECIOUS, THAN
TIME THAT A PARENT
SPENDS STRUGGLING
AND PONDERING WITH
GOD ON BEHALF OF
A CHILD.

MAX LUCADO

Hold your children before the Lord
in fervent prayer throughout their years
at home. There is no other source of
confidence and wisdom in parenting.
The God who made your children
will hear your petitions.
He has promised to do so.

JAMES DOBSON

I remember my mother, my father and
the rest of us praying together each evening.
It is God's greatest gift to the family.

MOTHER TERESA

Prayer is never the least we can do;
it is always the most!

A.W. TOZER

The most effective thing we can do for
our children and families is to pray for them.

ANTHONY EVANS

Prayer guards hearts and minds and causes
God to bring peace out of chaos.

BETH MOORE

Pour out your heart to God and tell Him
how you feel. Be real, be honest, and
when you get it all out, you'll start to feel
the gradual covering of
God's comforting presence.

BILL HYBELS

LET THE WORDS
OF MY MOUTH AND
THE MEDITATION OF
MY HEART BE
ACCEPTABLE IN
YOUR SIGHT, O LORD,
MY STRENGTH
AND MY REDEEMER.

PSALM 19:14 NKJV

I have found the perfect antidote for fear.
Whenever it sticks up its ugly face,
I clobber it with prayer.

DALE EVANS ROGERS

No man can do a great and enduring work
for God who is not a man of prayer, and
no man can be a man of prayer
who does not give much time to praying.

E. M. BOUNDS

To talk to his children about God,
a man needs to first talk to God
about his children.

EDWIN LOUIS COLE

I live in the spirit of prayer; I pray as I walk,
when I lie down, and when I rise.
And, the answers are always coming.

GEORGE MUELLER

Prayer connects us with
God's limitless potential.

HENRY BLACKABY

It is impossible to overstate the need
for prayer in the fabric of family life.

JAMES DOBSON

Pray, and let God worry.

MARTIN LUTHER

Thank You for . . .

DEMONSTRATING DISCIPLINE

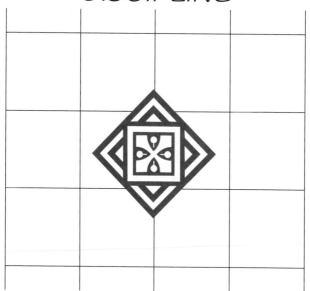

But I discipline my body and bring it
into subjection, lest, when I have preached to
others, I myself should become disqualified.

1 CORINTHIANS 9:27 NKJV

DEAR DAD,

Thanks for demonstrating discipline. When we were younger, you had the thankless task of controlling kids who would prefer not to be controlled. When we needed discipline, you provided it.

You taught me that disciplined behavior is a prerequisite for success. It's a lesson that never grows old. I'm still learning it, and you're still helping.

THE BIBLE CALLS FOR DISCIPLINE AND RECOGNITION OF AUTHORITY. CHILDREN MUST LEARN THIS AT HOME.

BILLY GRAHAM

Man's great danger is the combination of
his increased control over the elements
and his lack of control over himself.

ALBERT SCHWEITZER

No horse gets anywhere until he is harnessed.
No life ever grows great until it is focused,
dedicated, disciplined.

HARRY EMERSON FOSDICK

Have a profound respect for discipline.

SHUG JORDAN

Loving a child doesn't mean giving in to all
his whims; to love him is to bring out
the best in him, to teach him to love
what is difficult.

NADIA BOULANGER

Parental warmth after discipline is essential
to demonstrate that it is the behavior,
not the child himself, that the parent rejects.

JAMES DOBSON

The alternative to discipline is disaster.

VANCE HAVNER

The effective Christians of history have been
men and women of great personal discipline—
mental discipline, discipline of the body,
discipline of the tongue,
and discipline of the emotion.

BILLY GRAHAM

The goal of disciplining our children is
to encourage their growth as respectful,
responsible, self-disciplined individuals.

DON H. HIGHLANDER

The only lasting force of discipline
is self-discipline.

DALE BROWN

YOU CANNOT BE
DISCIPLINED
IN GREAT THINGS
AND UNDISCIPLINED
IN SMALL THINGS.

GEORGE S. PATTON

BY CONSTANT
SELF-DISCIPLINE
AND SELF-CONTROL,
YOU CAN DEVELOP
GREATNESS OF
CHARACTER

෨ං

GRENVILLE KLEISER

No steam or river ever drives anything
until it is confined. No Niagara is ever turned
into light and power until it is harnessed.

HARRY EMERSON FOSDICK

Some people regard discipline as a chore.
For me, it is a kind of order that
sets me free to fly.

JULIE ANDREWS

Without self-discipline, success is impossible.
Period.

LOU HOLTZ

LOVE YOUR CHILDREN
WITH ALL YOUR HEARTS;
LOVE THEM ENOUGH
TO DISCIPLINE THEM
BEFORE IT IS TOO LATE.

LAVINA CHRISTENSEN FUGAL

When we teach ourselves and our children
discipline, we are teaching them and
ourselves how to suffer and also how to grow.

M. SCOTT PECK

I've never known a man worth his salt who,
in the long run, deep down in his heart,
didn't appreciate the grind, the discipline.
I firmly believe that any man's finest hour,
this greatest fulfillment to all he holds dear,
is that moment he has worked his heart out
in a good cause and lies exhausted
on the field of battle, victorious.

VINCE LOMBARDI

Most true happiness comes from
one's inner life, from the disposition of
the mind and soul. Admittedly, a good inner life
is difficult to achieve, especially in these
trying times. It takes reflection
and contemplation and self-discipline.

W. L. SHIRER

Self-discipline is an acquired asset.

DUKE ELLINGTON

Diligence is the mother of good luck
and God gives all things to industry.

BEN FRANKLIN

Thank You for . . .
INSPIRING EXCELLENCE

While it is daytime, we must continue doing
the work of the One who sent me.
Night is coming, when no one can work.

JOHN 9:4 NCV

DEAR DAD,

Thank you for setting high standards. Had you not done so, I would have suffered. If less had been required of me, I would have responded with less effort. But, because you demanded more, I gave more. And I learned so very much from my hard work.

You taught me that excellence requires effort. And because you were willing to teach that lesson, I was compelled to learn it.

I PRAY NOT FOR VICTORY, BUT TO DO MY BEST.

AMOS ALONZO STAGG

I learned from my father how to work.
I learned from him that work is life
and life is work, and work is hard.

PHILIP ROTH

We must trust as if it all depended on God
and work as if it all depended on us.

C. H. SPURGEON

There is a silent dignity,
a fundamental usefulness,
and a primeval necessity in work.

FATHER FLANAGAN

Don't focus on being the best;
focus on doing your best.

DENIS WAITLEY

Thank God every morning when you get up
that you have something which must be done,
whether you like it or not. Work breeds
a hundred virtues that idleness never knows.

CHARLES KINGSLEY

It may be that the day of judgment will dawn
tomorrow; in that case, we shall gladly stop
working for a better tomorrow. But not before.

DIETRICH BONHOEFFER

Ordinary work, which is what
most of us do most of the time,
is ordained by God every bit
as much as is the extraordinary.

ELISABETH ELLIOT

I long to accomplish a great and noble task,
but it is my chief duty to accomplish small tasks
as if they were great and noble.

HELEN KELLER

You can't climb to the next rung on the ladder
until you are excellent at what you do now.

HARVEY MACKAY

First, we will be best; then we will be first.

LOU HOLTZ

Hands are made for work,
and the heart is made for God.

JOSEPHA ROSSELLO

Think enthusiastically about everything,
especially your work.

NORMAN VINCENT PEALE

The world does not consider labor a blessing,
therefore it flees and hates it,
but the pious who fear the Lord labor
with a ready and cheerful heart,
for they know God's command,
and they acknowledge His calling.

MARTIN LUTHER

Dear Lord, let us pray for our daily bread,
but let us not be afraid to hunt for it
with sweat running down the hoe handle.

SAM JONES

Let us work as if success depends on us alone,
but with the heartfelt conviction that
we are doing nothing and God everything.

ST. IGNATIUS LOYOLA

You will always have joy in the evening
if you spend the day fruitfully.

THOMAS À KEMPIS

Do everything for the love of God
and His glory without looking at the outcome
of the undertaking. Work is judged,
not by its result, but by its intention.

PADRE PIO OF PIETRELCINA

The things, good Lord, that I pray for,
give me the grace to labor for.

ST. THOMAS MORE

Do your work with your whole heart,
and you will succeed—
there is so little competition.

ELBERT HUBBARD

The higher the ideal, the more work is required
to accomplish it. Do not expect
to become a great success in life
if you are not willing to work for it.

FATHER FLANAGAN

I know of no more encouraging fact
than the unquestionable ability of man to
elevate his life by conscious endeavor.

HENRY DAVID THOREAU

Thank You for ...

MODELING
TRUE SUCCESS

His lord said to him, "Well done, good and
faithful servant; you were faithful over a few
things, I will make you ruler over many things.
Enter into the joy of your lord."

MATTHEW 25:21 NKJV

DEAR DAD,

Thanks for showing me what it means to be truly successful. As you know, genuine success has little to do with fame or fortune; it has everything to do with love, life, family, and faith. You're a wonderful example of what it means to be a fabulous father. Your legacy has touched our family and blessed our lives, and *that's* the real meaning of success.

SUCCESS USUALLY
COMES TO THOSE
WHO ARE TOO BUSY
TO BE LOOKING FOR IT.

HENRY DAVID THOREAU

There are no secrets to success:
Don't waste time looking for them.
Success is the result of perfection, hard work,
learning from failure, loyalty to those
for whom you work, and persistence.

COLIN POWELL

There's not much you can't achieve or endure
if you know God is walking by your side.
Just remember: Someone knows,
and Someone cares.

BILL HYBELS

People judge us by the success of our efforts.
God looks at the efforts themselves.

CHARLOTTE BRONTË

God's never been guilty of sponsoring a flop.

ETHEL WATERS

We, as believers, must allow God
to define success. And, when we do,
God blesses us with His love and His grace.

JIM GALLERY

Success or failure can be pretty well predicted
by the degree to which the heart is fully in it.

JOHN ELDREDGE

Often, attitude is the only difference between
success and failure.

JOHN MAXWELL

Success isn't the key. Faithfulness is.

JONI EARECKSON TADA

The secret of success is to find a need and fill it,
to find a hurt and heal it, to find somebody
with a problem and offer to help solve it.

ROBERT SCHULLER

SUCCESS AND HAPPINESS
ARE NOT DESTINATIONS.
THEY ARE EXCITING,
NEVER-ENDING
JOURNEYS.

ZIG ZIGLAR

Success is simple. Do what's right,
the right way, at the right time.

ARNOLD H. GLASGOW

The secret of success is constancy of purpose.

BENJAMIN DISRAELI

The world is moving so fast these days
that the man who says it can't be done
is generally interrupted
by someone doing it.

ELBERT HUBBARD

Success is finishing what God gave you to do.

HAROLD COOK

Success without honor is an unseasoned dish.

LOU HOLTZ

To find his place and fill it is success for a man.

PHILLIPS BROOKS

Enthusiasm is one of the most powerful engines
of success. When you do a thing, do it with
your might. Put your whole soul into it.
Be active, be energetic, be enthusiastic
and faithful. Nothing great was
ever achieved without enthusiasm.

RALPH WALDO EMERSON

The only thing that stands between a man
and what he wants from life is often merely
the will to try it and the faith to believe
that it is possible.

RICHARD M. DEVOS

If you want to be successful,
it's just this simple: Know what you're doing.
Love what you're doing.
And believe in what you're doing.

WILL ROGERS

Thank You for . . .

BEING A MAN
OF PURPOSE

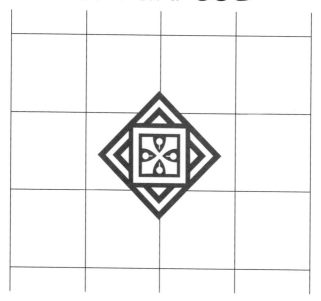

There is one thing I always do.
Forgetting the past and straining toward
what is ahead, I keep trying to reach the goal
and get the prize for which God called me . . . .

PHILIPPIANS 3:13, 14 NCV

DEAR DAD,

Thank you for showing me the power of purpose. Thank you teaching me that each day holds countless opportunities to build a better life and to make a better world. Thanks for helping me aim high; thanks for encouraging me to work hard; and thanks for teaching me to believe in myself.

By your words and your actions, you have shown me that God has a plan for all of us, including me. With God's help—and your encouragement—I, like you, will live a life of significance and purpose.

HAPPINESS MEANS
HAVING SOMETHING
TO DO AND SOMETHING
TO LIVE FOR.

FULTON J. SHEEN

God custom-designed you with your unique
combination of personality, temperament,
talents, and background, and
He wants to harness and use these in
His mission to reach this messed-up world.

BILL HYBELS

Aim at Heaven and you will get earth
"thrown in"; aim at earth
and you will get neither.

C. S. LEWIS

Fear not that thy life shall come to an end,
but rather fear that it
shall never have a beginning.

CARDINAL NEWMAN

We aren't just thrown on this earth like
dice tossed across a table.
We are lovingly placed here for a purpose.

CHARLES SWINDOLL

Many people flounder about in life because
they have no purpose. Before it is possible to
achieve anything, an objective must be set.

GEORGE HALAS

Plunge boldly into the thick of life!

GOETHE

The strength and happiness of a man consists in
finding out the way in which God is going,
and going that way too.

HENRY WARD BEECHER

Blessed are those who know what on earth
they are here on earth to do and
set themselves about the business of doing it.

MAX LUCADO

We are all pencils in the hand of God.

MOTHER TERESA

Continually restate to yourself
what the purpose of your life is.

OSWALD CHAMBERS

Believe, when you are most unhappy,
that there is something for you to do in
the world. So long as you can sweeten
another's pain, life is not in vain.

HELEN KELLER

Let us live with urgency. Let us exploit
the opportunity of life. Let us not drift.
Let us live intentionally.
We must not trifle our lives away.

RAYMOND ORTLUND

You were made by God and for God——
and until you understand that,
life will not make sense.

RICK WARREN

LIFE IS GOD'S NOVEL.
LET HIM WRITE IT.

ISAAC BASHEVIS SINGER

Thank You for . . .
YOUR WISDOM

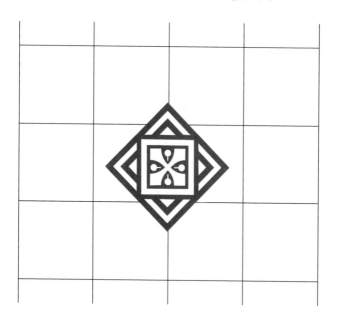

He will teach us His ways,
and we shall walk in His paths.

ISAIAH 2:3 NKJV

DEAR DAD,

Thanks for sharing your wisdom. For longer than I can remember, you've taught me life's most important lessons. You are the teacher, I am the pupil, and class is still in session.

One of life's great ironies is that there is so much to learn and so little time. That's why I value the lessons you have taught me *and* the ones that I still have to learn.

THE DOORS OF WISDOM ARE NEVER SHUT.

∽

BEN FRANKLIN

God's plan for our guidance is for us
to grow gradually in wisdom before
we get to the cross roads.

BILL HYBELS

Knowledge is horizontal.
Wisdom is vertical; it comes down from above.

BILLY GRAHAM

Don't expect wisdom to come into your life
like great chunks of rock on a conveyor belt.
Wisdom comes privately from God as
a byproduct of right decisions, godly reactions,
and the application of spiritual principles
to daily circumstances.

CHARLES SWINDOLL

A prudent question is one-half of wisdom.

FRANCIS BACON

Cleverness is not wisdom.

EURIPIDES

The more wisdom enters our hearts,
the more we will be able to trust our hearts
in difficult situations.

JOHN ELDREDGE

Patience is the companion of wisdom.

ST. AUGUSTINE

The Spirit of God is direct, authoritative,
the foundation of wisdom,
life, and holiness.

ST. JOHN OF DAMASCUS

Wisdom is the supreme part of happiness.

SOPHOCLES

LIFE IS A FESTIVAL ONLY TO THE WISE.

∽

RALPH WALDO EMERSON

IF WE WORK IN MARBLE,
IT WILL PERISH;
IF WE WORK UPON BRASS,
TIME WILL EFFACE IT;
IF WE REAR TEMPLES,
THEY WILL CRUMBLE INTO
DUST; BUT IF WE WORK
UPON IMMORTAL MINDS
AND INSTILL IN THEM JUST
PRINCIPLES, WE ARE THEN
ENGRAVING UPON TABLETS
WHICH NO TIME WILL EFFACE,
BUT WILL BRIGHTEN AND
BRIGHTEN TO ALL ETERNITY.

DANIEL WEBSTER

Thank You for ...
YOUR LOVE

Beloved, if God so loved us,
we also ought to love one another.

1 JOHN 4:11 NKJV

DEAR DAD,

A father's love is a gift that is freely given, a gift that is demonstrated by deed and word, a gift that begins before birth and endures forever.

Great dads come in a wide range of shapes, sizes, colors, temperaments and nationalities; but they all share a singular trait: paternal love. Sometimes, that devotion is tested to the limits: even well-intended children occasionally behave in ways that only a parent could love. Thankfully, you've forgiven my shortcomings, and for that, I'm grateful. Your heart is big enough to love me in of spite my imperfections . . . thank goodness, and bless you, Dad, forever!

HE WHO IS FILLED WITH LOVE IS FILLED WITH GOD HIMSELF.

∽

ST. AUGUSTINE

Love is a multiplication.

MARJORY STONEMAN DOUGLAS

When the evening of this life comes,
we shall be judged on love.

ST. JOHN OF THE CROSS

Whoever loves true life, will love true love.

ELIZABETH BARRETT BROWNING

Nobody has ever measured, not even poets,
how much the heart can hold.

ZELDA FITZGERALD

The best and most beautiful things in
the world cannot be seen or even touched.
They must be felt with the heart.

HELEN KELLER

Accustom yourself continually to make
many acts of love, for they enkindle
and melt the soul.

ST. TERESA OF AVILA

Love is not a state, it is a direction.

SIMONE WEIL

When a child is convinced he is greatly loved
and respected by his parents,
he is inclined to accept his own worth
as a person.

JAMES DOBSON

The giving of love is an education in itself.

ELEANOR ROOSEVELT

Love is ever the beginning of knowledge
as fire is of light.

THOMAS CARLYLE

To love is to receive a glimpse of heaven.

KAREN SUNDE

Nothing we do, however virtuous,
can be accomplished alone;
therefore we are saved by love.

REINHOLD NIEBUHR

Love is the essence of God.

RALPH WALDO EMERSON

Love stretches your heart
and makes you big inside.

MARGARET WALKER

Real love is a permanently
self-enlarging experience.

M. SCOTT PECK

There is no love which does not become help.

PAUL TILLICH

LOVE IS AN ACTIVE VERB—
A RIVER, NOT A POND.

ROBERT FULGHUM

THE BRAVEST ARE
THE TENDEREST.
THE LOVING ARE
THE DARING.

HENRY WADSWORTH LONGFELLOW

Love wins when everything else will fail.

FANNY JACKSON COPPIN

There is only one terminal dignity—
love.

HELEN HAYES

What the world really needs is more love
and less paperwork.

PEARL BAILEY

FOR THOSE WHO LOVE . . .
TIME IS ETERNITY.

HENRY VAN DYKE